BEAUTIFUL ORIGAMI

Zülal Aytüre-Scheele

Sterling Publishing Co., Inc.   New York

CONTENTS

Edited by Timothy Nolan
Photographs by ART TECH Photo-Design-Studio Gerhard Burrock, Wiesbaden-Naurod
Translated by Elisabeth E. Reinersmann

Library of Congress Cataloging-in-Publication Data

Aytüre-Scheele, Zülal.
    [Zauberwelt origami Tierfiguren aus Papier. English]
    Beautiful origami / by Zülal Aytüre-Scheele ; [edited by Timothy
Nolan ; translated by Elisabeth E. Reinersmann].
       p.   cm.
    Translation of: Zauberwelt origami Tierfiguren aus Papier.
    1. Origami.   I. Title.
    TT870.A9913   1990   90-9735
    736'.982—dc20   CIP

15 14 13 12

English translation © 1990 by Sterling Publishing Co., Inc.
387 Park Avenue South, New York, N.Y. 10016
Original edition published under the title *Zauberwelt Origami*
© 1989 by Falken-Verlag GmbH, 6272 Niedernhausen/Ts.
Distributed in Canada by Sterling Publishing
c/o Canadian Manda Group, One Atlantic Avenue, Suite 105
Toronto, Ontario, Canada M6K 3E7
Distributed in Great Britain and Europe by Chris Lloyd
at Orca Book Services, Stanley House, Fleets Lane,
Poole BH15 3AJ England
Distributed in Australia by Capricorn Ltd.
P.O. Box 704, Windsor, NSW 2756 Australia
Printed in China

Sterling ISBN 0-8069-7382-X Paper
           0-8069-7381-1 Trade

FOREWORD

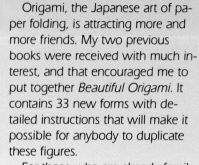

Origami, the Japanese art of paper folding, is attracting more and more friends. My two previous books were received with much interest, and that encouraged me to put together *Beautiful Origami*. It contains 33 new forms with detailed instructions that will make it possible for anybody to duplicate these figures.

For those who are already familiar with the technique of paper folding, it is no secret that origami is not simply a technique but really an art form. However, for the creation of new, artistic forms a certain expertise is imperative.

I hope that this book will increase the circle of origami friends. Origami is a magical world filled with creative imagination that everyone can discover while having fun with these projects.

Zülal Aytüre-Scheele

PAPER
AND
BASIC
RULES

The right choice of paper is very important for the successful outcome of your origami figures. Many gift and craft stores sell origami paper in different sizes and colors. But you can just as well use gift-wrapping paper cut to proper size. The paper should be strong enough to withstand repeated folding and handling so that it will not stretch or tear. Its surface must be flat, smooth, and thin, but strong. While the paper does not have to be of any size, it must be perfectly square. If you are familiar with origami, you won't have any problem choosing the right paper.

All figures that start out with the same basic steps are grouped together, with the instructions given at the beginning. This way, you will be able to get to know the systems that are the foundations of origami, as well as the steps necessary to create your own forms and figures.

For example, the lioness and Pegasus start out with identical steps and it is impossible to recognize in the beginning how different, with subsequently different folding steps, the final form will be. Knowledge of the systems that are the basis of origami is essential for the creation of new forms and figures.

Follow all instructions to the letter and keep in mind the last steps you did as you go on to the next. In order to achieve proper proportions of your figures, fold along the dashed lines exactly, and follow all additional information (for example: "Fold to the middle"). Ordinarily it is sufficient to follow the dashed lines on your form. But if you don't trust your eye or if you work with a particularly large size, measure the line and transfer it, in proportion, to your work.

The photos in this book are all in color to make your work easier. The photos of some of the more difficult steps have been enlarged to give a clear view of the necessary details.

In order to avoid any misunder-
standing, here is one of the basic
forms with terms used in the text:

Obviously, confusing left and
right, upper and lower, or front and
back just once will result in a totally
different form.

One of the most frequently used
terms (and one of the most important) is *open*. When opening a tip,
fold either the open or closed edge
to the inside or outside, respectively.
For example, after creasing a
dashed line (always the first step in
opening a tip), open the left tip up
as shown.

Most open tips will put the inner
edges on the inside, but there are
exceptions. It is important when
opening a tip to carefully look at the
photographs to double-check how
to open the particular tip.

2 ⚊ ⚊ 1

6. . . . fold wing up. Repeat on the other side. Cut line 1 as indicated to make the tail. Fold the tip of line 2 . . .

7. . . . to the inside to make the beak.

Carrier Pigeon

1. Crease a square piece of paper diagonally.

3. . . . to the right. Fold the top layer on the dashed line . . .

4. . . . to the left. Fold the upper portion of form . . .

8. Fold corners below the tail on dashed line . . .

2. Fold the paper once, diagonally (if paper is white on one side make sure it is on the inside, so the form is open on the left side. Fold the left corner . . .

5. . . . together in the middle. At dashed line . . .

9. . . . to the inside on both sides to finish your carrier pigeon.

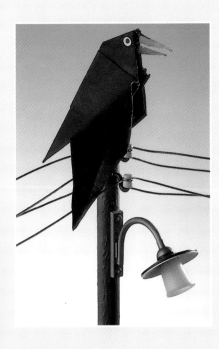

3. . . . to the inside and . . .

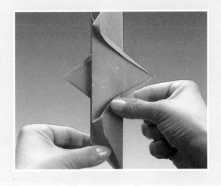

7. . . . to the middle.

Raven

4. . . . reinforce creases of both triangles.

1. Follow steps 1–3 for the carrier pigeon. Fold the right upper corner . . .

8. Reinforce the creases of the just created triangles and fold the form together in the middle.

1
2

9. Open the tip to the inside on dashed line 1 and fold the wings up on dashed line 2.

5. Pull the right triangle forward.

6. Fold the edges of the right triangle on dashed line . . .

2. . . . to the left. Fold the edges of this triangle on the dashed line as indicated . . .

10. Fold both wings down on the dashed line and your raven is sitting pretty.

7. On the dashed line . . .

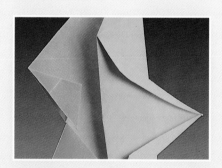

8. . . . crease both the tips up . . .

Bat

9. . . . and then down.

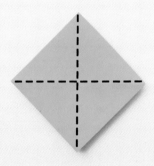

1. Crease a square piece of paper diagonally as marked.

4. . . . to the middle and flatten down both small triangles.

2. Fold the square diagonally in half. Fold the left tip to the right.

5. Cut as indicated on dashed line . . .

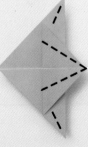

3. . . . Fold all edges as marked, outer edges first . . .

6. . . . and fold the tips back.

10. Lift each tip and press together as shown.

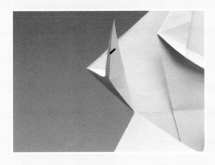

11. Press form down to flatten. Fold the dashed line . . .

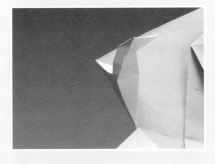

12. . . . to the right; then upwards and downwards, respectively. These are the bat's feet.

13. Turn the form over.

14. Fold form to- gether in the middle.

15. Fold the front wing on dashed line . . .

16. Turn the form over and repeat. Fold the dashed line . . .

17. . . . down along the upper tips . . .

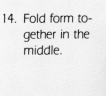

18. . . . on both sides.

19. Unfold steps 17 and 18. Fold both tips along the dashed line . . .

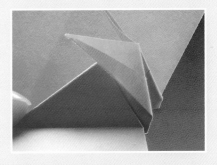

20. . . . forward and backwards, respectively.

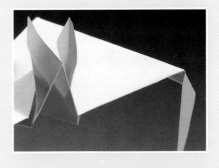

21. Shape both tips into ears.

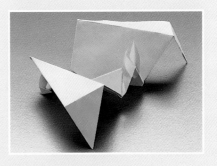

22. Fold the feet of your bat down.

7. . . . as shown.

Owl

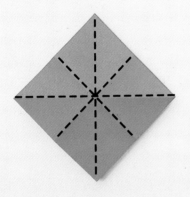

1. Crease a square piece of paper along the dashed lines.

4. Open this half and flatten it.

8. Slowly open the front wing at lower tip.

2. Fold the paper in half.

5. Repeat this procedure on the other side. Crease the right and left edges of the top portion (the wing) . . .

9. Push the left and right corners down at the middle.

3. Lift up the right half of triangle horizontally.

6. . . . to the middle. Crease the upper tip down . . .

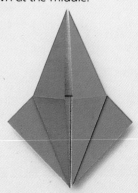

10. Press the form down firmly.

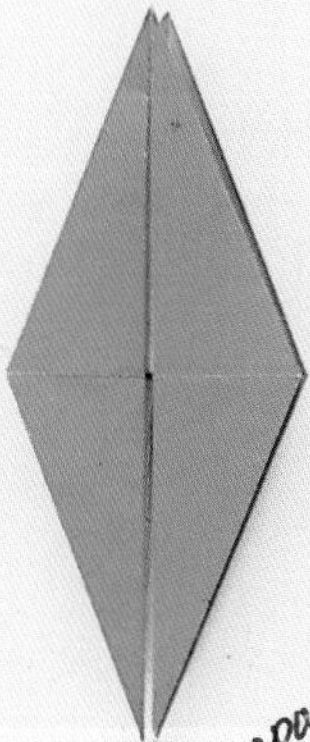

separation: both sides on middle layer

11. Turn the form over and repeat steps 1–6.

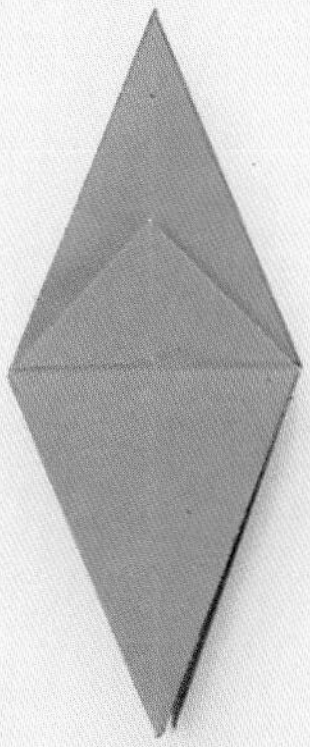

12. Fold the upper tip down to the lower tip.

13. Turn the form over and repeat. Fold the dashed line . . .

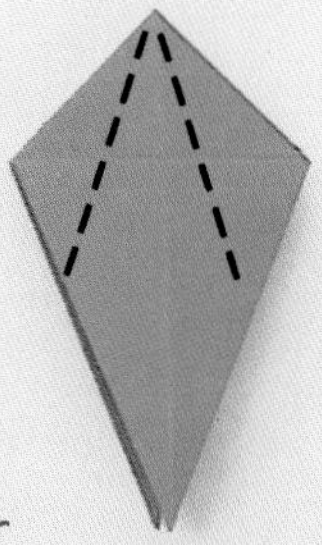

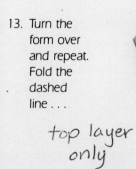

top layer only

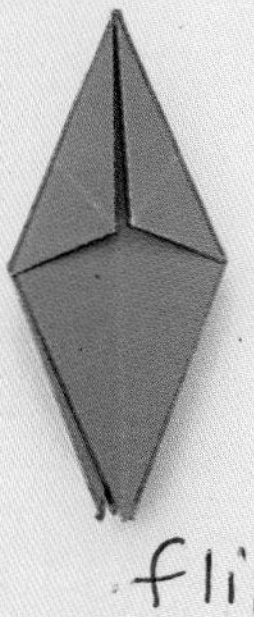

flip,

14. . . . to the middle. Repeat on the other side.

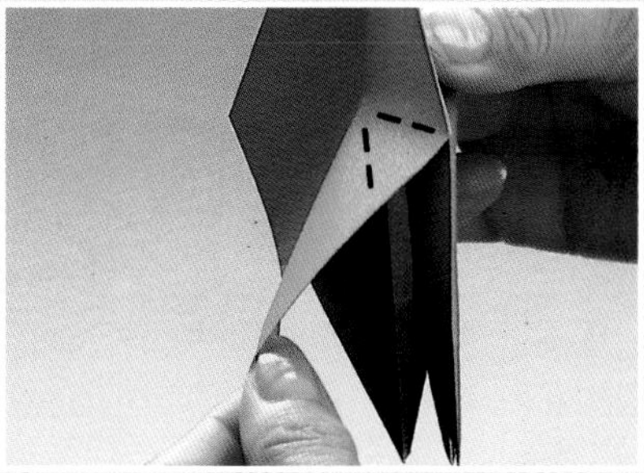

15. Lift up the left inner wing. Fold on the dashed line . . .

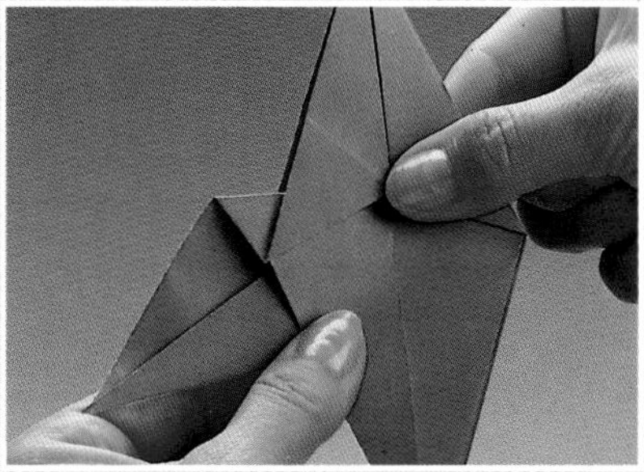

16. . . . and press together.

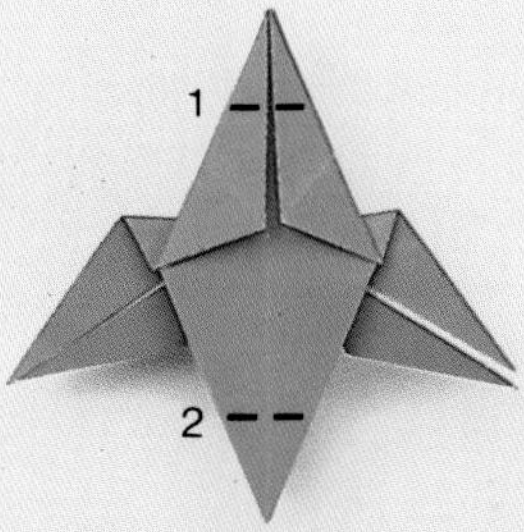

17. Repeat on the other side; then fold down dashed line 1. Fold dashed line 2 . . .

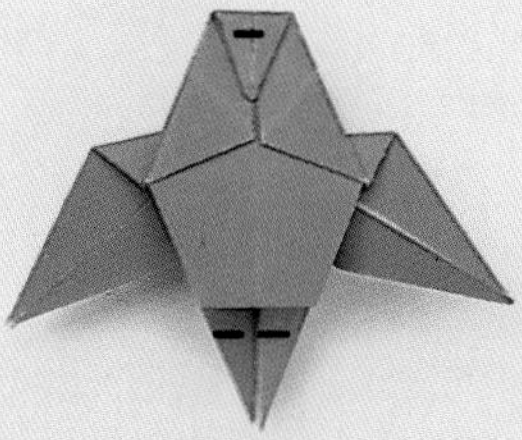

inside

18. . . . up. Fold the dashed lines . . .

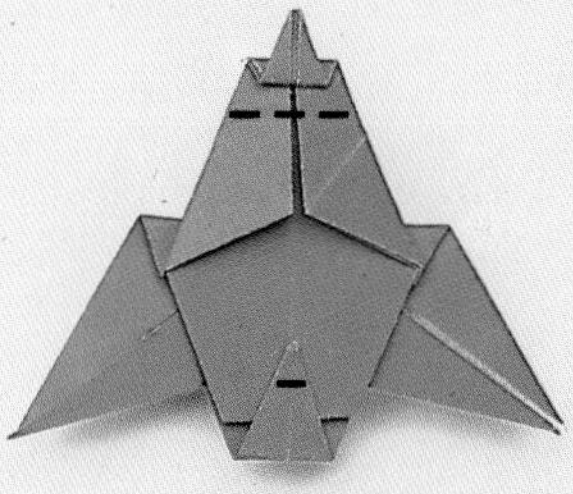

19. . . . of the head and tail up. On the dashed line . . .

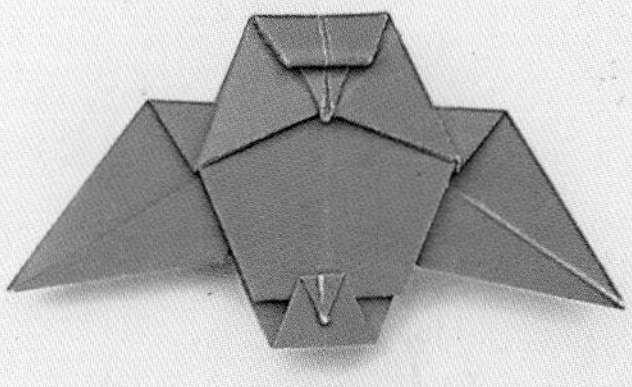

20. . . . fold the upper portion of head and the lower tip of the tail down. Turn the form over.

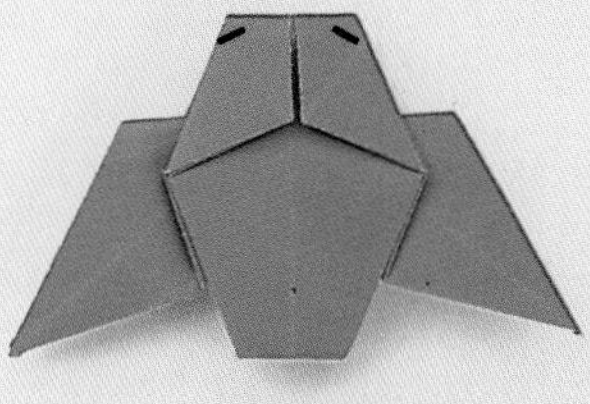

21. Cut the paper at the mark on the head. Turn figure over.

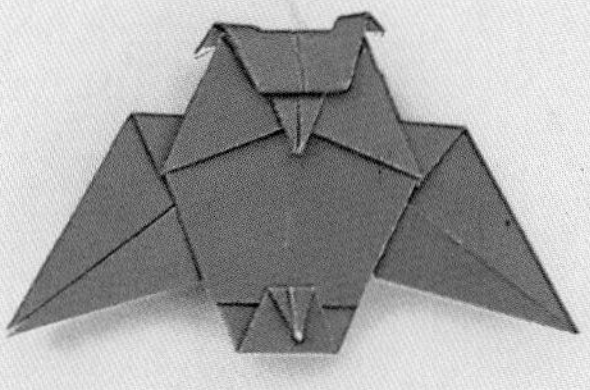

22. Shape the ears and your owl is ready to fly.

Flying Stork

7. . . . on top of the right tip. Turn the form and repeat steps 4–7. Fold the dashed line . . .

8. . . . as shown—back to the left. Turn the form over and repeat this step. Fold the lower edge of dashed line 1 . . .

1. Follow steps 1–10 of the Owl (pages 14–15); then, with the open tip pointing to the left, fold both edges of right top wing . . .

4. Fold the right tip . . .

9. . . . upwards. Turn the right tip up on line 2, then open left tip on dashed line . . .

2. . . . to the middle. Fold the upper portion of the wing . . .

5. . . . on top of the left tip. Fold the upper wing . . .

3. . . . down. Turn the form over.

6. . . . down. Fold the left front tip . . .

10. . . . and turn up as shown.

11. Open left tip of dashed line 1 . . .

12. . . . to the left. Open the right tip of dashed line 2 . . .

13. . . . to the right. On dashed line 3 open the tip again to the left.

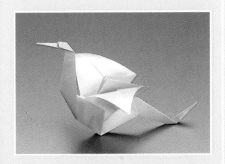

14. This is your stork in flight.

Standing Stork

1. Follow steps 1–11 of the Owl (pages 14–15). Have the open tip pointing to the left.

2. Crease as marked.

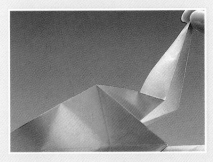

3. Open the right upper tip and open it up at the crease.

4. Open the right lower tip down.

5. Open both points and fold front half to the left. Fold the dashed lines . . .

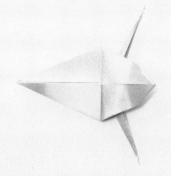

6. . . . twice to the left along right edge and three times to the right on the left edge.

10. Fold the left front wing to the right at the middle crease; then turn the form over.

14. . . . open the left tip and turn it up at the crease as shown.

15. Crease the tips to shape feet and neck along the dashed line.

7. Fold the dashed line . . .

11. Fold the edges of the wings on the dashed lines . . .

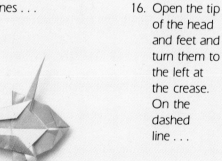

16. Open the tip of the head and feet and turn them to the left at the crease. On the dashed line . . .

8. . . . to the right along the left upper tip. Fold both corners along the dashed line . . .

12. . . . to the middle. Fold the form together.

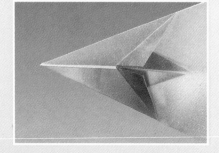

9. . . . towards the horizontal midline.

13. Crease along the dashed lines; then . . .

17. . . . fold the left corner inside. Shape the beak according to steps 11–14 for the Flying Stork (page 16).

7. . . . and turn crease 2 . . .

Dove

8. . . . down. Open the wings . . .

1. Crease a piece of paper as shown.

4. . . . together in the middle. Crease on dashed line 1.

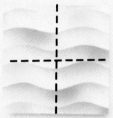

9. . . . on both sides and glue the inner edges together.

2. Fold the upper left and lower left corners to the middle (keep the white side inside).

5. Fold lower right corner at the crease to the inside. Fold both upper corners on dashed line 2 . . .

3. Fold the right portion of the form in an accordion fold to the middle as shown. Fold form . . .

6. . . . down on both sides as shown. Crease the form on dashed lines 1 and 2. Open the left corner up at crease 1 . . .

10. Spread the wings apart and let your dove fly.

Sea Lion

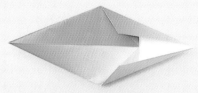

4. Unfold step 3.

7. Fold the small wing to the right and the lower half of form . . .

8. . . . backwards. At the dashed line, fold . . .

1. Crease a square piece of paper diagonally.

5. Lift both inner corners so that they meet in the middle. Fold them upright . . .

9. . . . the small wing on both sides to the left. Crease both dashed lines· and . . .

2. Fold the left edges to the middle (keep the white side inside).

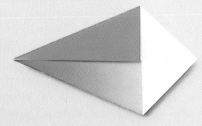

3. Fold right edges to the middle.

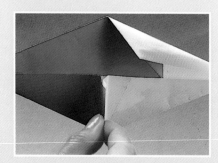

6. . . . and push both sides together. Press it down firmly.

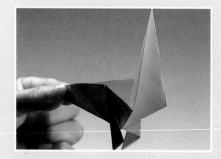

10. . . . open the right tip up at the crease.

11. Open the left tip up at the crease and fold it a little to the inside. Crease the dashed line . . .

12. . . . and open the left tip to the right. Cut the beak up at the lower edge about one third of the length of the head.

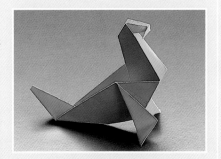

13. Open both tips backwards and forward respectively. This is the "beard" of your sea lion.

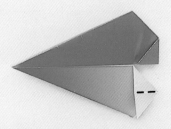

14. Fold his legs slightly and set him down.

Whale

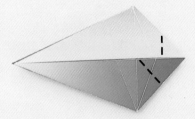

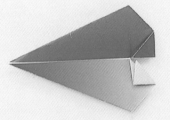

1. Follow steps 1–7 of the Sea Lion (page 22).

2. Fold upper right half of the form in the middle backwards. Turn form over. Fold the lower tip down at the dashed line . . .

3. . . . and the right upper tip left to the middle. Fold the dashed line . . .

4. . . . up at the lower tip.

5. Slowly fold the upper half of form on top of the lower. At the same time, fold the upper small triangle into the lower one . . .

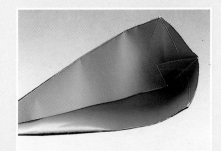

6. . . . and push it against the upper half. Glue both portions together as shown.

7. Fold the form together. Crease the dashed lines. Fold the left tip . . .

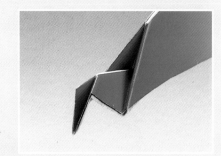

11. Open both tips down on crease 1.

Shark

1. Follow steps 1–7 of the Sea Lion (page 22); then fold the tip of the wings at the dashed lines.

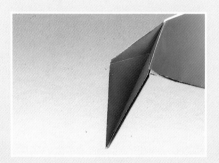

8. . . . down on crease 1 and . . .

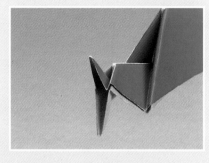

12. Open only the upper tip on crease 2.

2. Fold the tip on the right to the left, along the dashed line.

9. . . . to the left on crease 2.

13. Open the lower edges on both sides in at dashed line. This is the tummy of the whale. All you need to do now is . . .

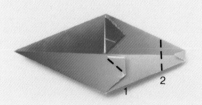

3. On dashed line 1 crease lower triangle. On dashed line 2 . . .

10. Crease both dashed lines.

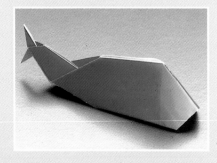

14. . . . shape the body.

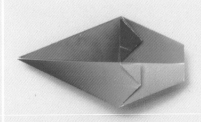

4. . . . fold the right tip backwards.

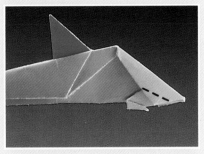

10. Fold both corners up on the dashed line . . .

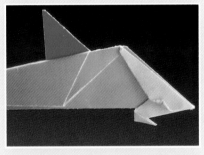

11. . . . on both sides. Pull the lower tip down as shown.

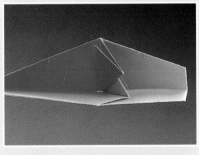

5. Slowly fold the lower half of the form on top of the upper left. At the same time, open the small lower triangle . . .

7. Press form together. Fold the dashed line . . .

8. . . . down on both sides. Fold the dashed line . . .

12. At the dashed line . . .

13. . . . open the left tip up.

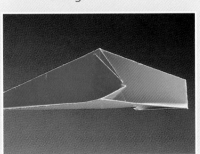

6. . . . behind the upper small triangle.

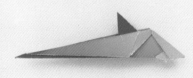

9. . . . back along the corners.

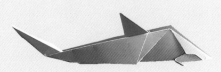

14. Your shark is ready to take to the waters.

Ray

1. Start with a square piece of paper.

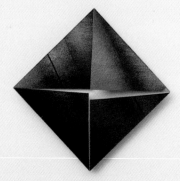

2. Fold all four corners to the middle as shown. Keep the white side inside.

3. Turn the form over.

4. Fold the left edges to the middle; then . . .

5. . . . fold the short right edges there as well.

6. Undo the last two folds; then lift up both inner edges, push them together and . . .

7. . . . fold to the right.

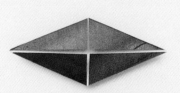

8. Turn the form over.

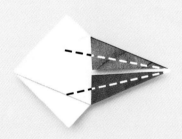

9. Open both "wings" on the left and fold the dashed lines . . .

10. . . . to the middle. Fold the dashed lines . . .

11. . . . again to the middle. Fold dashed line 1 . . .

12. . . . to the right, and fold line 2 back to the left again.

13. Turn form over. Cut as indicated on the dashed lines.

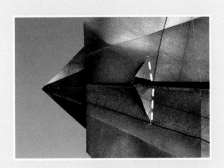

14. Fold the tips on the dashed lines . . .

15. . . . to the right. Open the tips . . .

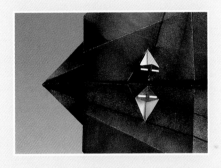

16. . . . and flatten them as shown. On both dashed lines . . .

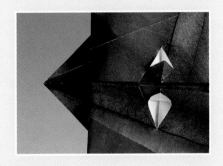

17. . . . lift up the "eyes."

18. Push the tail together and give it a wavy look.

THE MEADOW

3. Cut *only* the top layer along the dashed line.

7. Push them together, and fold back, tucking in the smaller triangle to form a tip.

4. Fold the left edges horizontally to the middle. Fold the right sides . . .

8. Fold both dashed lines . . .

Turtle

1. Follow steps 1–8 of the Ray (page 26) (make sure you start out with the colored side of the paper inside).

5. . . . to the midline as well.

9. . . . to the right, and the two "white" triangles across the midline.

2. Open right and left portion of form; and turn it over.

6. Undo steps 4–5 and lift up both edges at the midline as shown.

10. Fold the far right tip a little to the left. Cut the upper layers along dashed lines (as in step 3).

11. Repeat steps 3–9 with the right portion of the form.

15. Fold it down to the left.

19. Reinforce the small triangles . . .

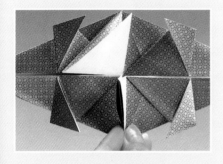

12. Lift the lower small (white) triangle.

16. Repeat steps 12–15 with the upper triangle. Fold dashed lines 1 to the middle and . . .

20. . . . that were just created. This is the turtle's tail.

13. Fold the right outer layer . . .

17. . . . 2 back to the outside. Fold the dashed lines . . .

21. Turn the form over.

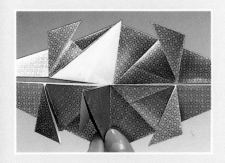

14. . . . over to the left side.

18. . . . to the middle.

22. Lift head and upright legs.

5. . . . lift up both corners and push them to the outside. At the same time . . .

Butterfly

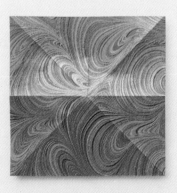

1. Crease a square piece of paper horizontally and diagonally.

3. Fold the left and right edges to the middle, vertically. Turn the form over.

6. . . . fold the left edge to the middle.

2. Fold the top and bottom edges to the middle. (Keep the white side inside.)

4. Unfold step 3. At dashed line . . .

7. Repeat for the right side.

8. Fold left tips over to the left.

11. . . . the left half of the form over to the right.

12. Fold the upper half back as shown. Fold the dashed line . . .

15. . . . push the lower corner inside.

9. Fold the dashed lines . . .

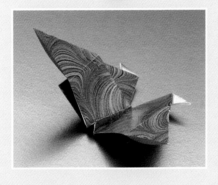

13. . . . on both sides up at the crease.

16. Repeat on the other side.

10. . . . up. At the middle, fold . . .

14. At the dashed line . . .

17. Unfold the form.

5. Fold one half of the open tip to the left, and the other to the right.

6. Fold along the upper dashed line while pulling the tip . . .

Dragonfly

1. Follow steps 1–10 of the Owl (pages 14–15). The open corners should be on the left.

3. Slowly pull the tips of the right portion apart until . . .

7. . . . upwards vertically.

2. Fold the top and bottom corners to the middle. Turn the form over and repeat.

4. . . . a small square is formed. Hold the sides carefully. You should now have a "T" shape.

8. Open it up, and flatten it.

9. Repeat steps 6–8 on the left lower corner, as shown.

12. Fold the lower portion of the form back.

15. Open up left tip and roll up paper as shown: this is the head.

10. Turn form over. Fold the dashed lines . . .

13. Cut along dashed line 1 to create wings. Open the left and right corners down on lines 2 and 3.

16. Open the wings.

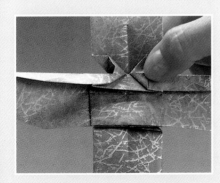

11. . . . to the middle horizontally and smooth out all the small triangles as shown.

14. Lift at dashed line and push it towards the wings.

17. Fold all four wingtips to give them shape.

7. Fold both upper edges to the midline. Fold the dashed lines . . .

Scorpion

8. . . . stairfashion, as shown. Fold the dashed lines . . .

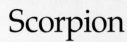

1. Start with a triangular piece of paper (cut a square piece in half diagonally). Fold the dashed lines . . .

4. Fold back the left half of the form.

9. . . . right and left, respectively. Fold dashed line 1 . . .

5. Repeat with the right half.

2. . . . to the top corner (keep the white side inside). Fold the dashed lines . . .

10. . . . down. Fold dashed line 2 up and dashed line 3 down. Fold the dashed lines . . .

3. . . . down to the vertical midline.

6. Fold down both upper tips, tucking in both small triangles the folds will create.

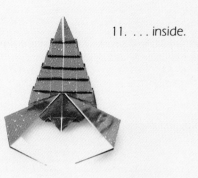

11. . . . inside.

12. Turn form over. Open the tips on the dashed lines . . .

13. . . . to the outside.

14. Fold form together in the middle and slowly pull up back portion.

Grasshopper

1. Follow steps 1–5 of the Scorpion (page 36). Cut along the dashed lines.

2. Point the cut portion to the left.

3. Fold back upper portion of form at the midline. Fold the dashed line . . .

4. . . . up. Fold the right upper edge along the dashed line . . .

5. . . . to form the wing. Repeat on back wing. Fold both edges along the dashed line . . .

6. . . . to the inside. Fold both edges along the dashed line . . .

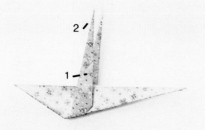

7. . . . to the inside on both sides.

11. Fold down on line 1 . . .

Amaryllis

1. Start with three rectangular pieces of paper, each two-thirds as wide as it is long. Fold all three pieces as shown, with all four corners down, and the white side of the paper inside.

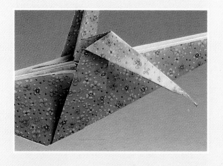

8. Open up the tip and fold down on line 1; then fold . . .

12. . . . fold up on line 2, . . .

2. Fold the upper and lower edges to the middle.

9. . . . to the right on line 2. Repeat procedure on the other side.

13. and down on line 3 again.

3. Fold each piece in half.

10. Crease along dashed lines.

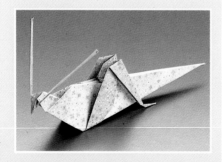

14. Your grasshopper is ready for action.

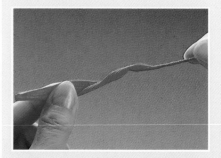

4. Take some crepe paper, twist it into small roles and insert it into each form. Round out the ends.

Magnolia

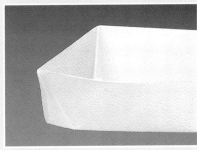

4. Pinch all four corners inside as shown.

5. Fold back upper portion of form.

6. Repeat steps 2–5 with the other two pieces of paper. Put all three pieces next to each other and crease in the middle.

7. Attach a piece of wire at the crease and twist it at the bottom. Shape flower.

1. Start with three rectangular pieces of paper, each two-thirds as wide as it is long. Crease each in the middle.

2. Fold the upper and lower edges to the middle.

3. Crease all four corners to the middle.

5. Put all three forms together, crease them in the middle, and bind them together with a piece of wire, twisting it at the bottom as shown.

6. Glue the petals together, open them up and give your flower a pretty shape.

Chrysanthemum

5. Reinforce all your folds.

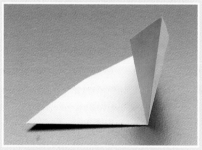

6. Turn the form over and repeat the procedure on the other side. Crease the upper folds along the dashed lines to the middle.

1. Crease a square piece of paper horizontally, vertically and diagonally.

3. Lift up one half of the triangle, open it, and . . .

7. Lift up, open and flatten . . .

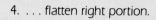

2. Fold along one diagonal crease.

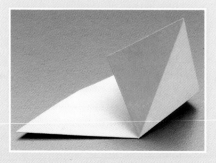

4. . . . flatten right portion.

8. . . . the upper right wing (the one you just folded). Fold this new small wing . . .

9. . . . to the right.

13. Fold the right wing to the left and fold the upper tip down (as in step 12).

17. . . . down as shown.

10. Repeat procedure with left wing.

14. Do the same on the other side.

18. Gently pull the petals and shape the flower.

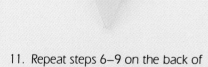

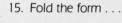

11. Repeat steps 6–9 on the back of the form. Fold the dashed line . . .

15. Fold the form . . .

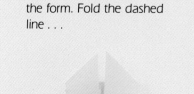

12. . . . down on the upper tip only. Repeat on the other side.

16. . . . in the middle. Fold the dashed line . . .

19. Your chrysanthemum is finished.

THE JUNGLE

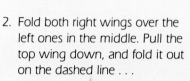

2. Fold both right wings over the left ones in the middle. Pull the top wing down, and fold it out on the dashed line . . .

5. . . . to the middle (top edges only). Fold all the dashed lines . . .

3. . . . as shown.

6. . . . forward to the middle.

Giraffe

1. Follow steps 1–11 of the Owl (pages 14–15). Point the open tip upwards.

4. Fold the top wing over. Fold the dashed line . . .

7. Fold right half over to the left. Fold the dashed line . . .

8. . . . down to the right. Fold dashed lines 1 and 2 . . .

9. . . . forward and backwards on both sides. Push dashed line 1 . . .

10. . . . inside and up to dashed line 2.

11. Open the upper tip on line 1 . . .

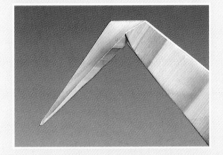

12. . . . to the left and . . .

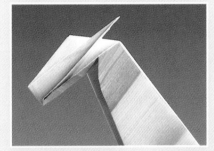

13. . . . open line 2 to the outside and up.

14. Cut tip as shown.

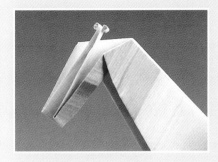

15. Roll both ends up slightly and push . . .

16. . . . both upper corners down to form the ears.

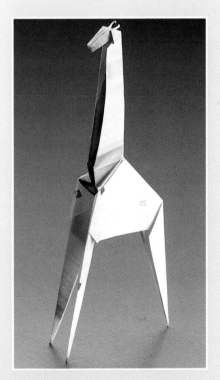

17. Your giraffe is ready to inspect his territory.

Crocodile

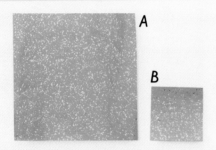

Two square pieces of paper are needed. Piece B should be about one third the size of piece A.

Body

1. Using paper A, follow steps 1–11 of the Owl (pages 14–15). Point the open tip to the right. Cut along the dashed lines . . .

2. . . . into the wings as shown.

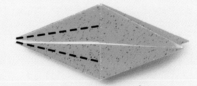

3. Fold along the dashed lines . . .

4. . . . both edges to the horizontal midline. Fold this new wing along the dashed lines . . .

5. . . . to the right tip.

6. Turn the form over. Fold on the dashed lines . . .

7. . . . to the horizontal middle. Fold the right tips on the dashed lines . . .

8. . . . to the left; then fold the dashed lines . . .

Head

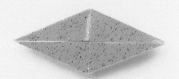

9. . . . up as shown.

10. Open the lower portion of the tip up to the crease; this should give you a rhomboid shape.

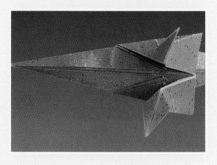

11. Pull the tips a little to the right and flatten the form.

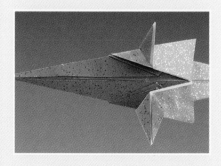

12. Fold the dashed lines . . .

13. . . . to the middle; then on the dashed lines . . .

14. . . . turn them up.

15. Turn form over. Fold the dashed line . . .

16. . . . to the right.

17. Use paper B and follow steps 1–11 of the Owl (pages 14–15). Point the open tip to the left. Pull both right tips . . .

18. . . . apart, until . . .

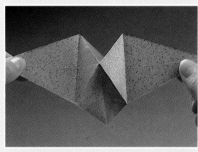

19. . . . the paper is flat.

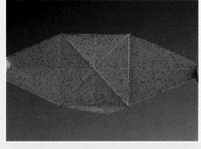

20. Turn paper over. Push along the dashed lines . . .

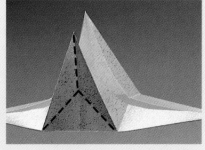

21. . . . so both tips come together until they are flat.

22. Fold both tips over to the left side. Crease the dashed line . . .

23. . . . as shown.

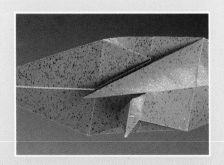

24. Open lower portion of tip up to the crease.

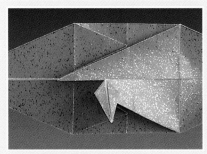

25. Pull tip a little to the right, flatten, and glue to the surface underneath.

26. Repeat steps 22–25 with the upper tip. These are the eyes. Fold both dashed lines . . .

27. . . . back. Push the head into the body up to the dashed lines . . .

28. . . . and glue in place.

29. Push form together until the mouth opens.

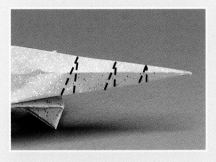

30. Crease the dashed lines . . .

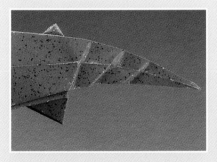

31. . . . and fold them to give the tail its slightly bent form.

32. Open the legs backwards slightly.

6. . . . and open tip to the left. Crease again at the dashed line and open at that point to the outside. This is the head.

7. To make the tail, crease dashed lines 1 and 2.

8. Open the tail down on line 1 and . . .

9. . . . up on line 2.

Snake

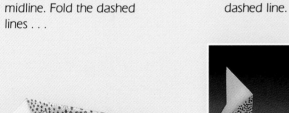

3. . . . once more to the middle.

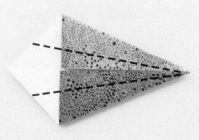

1. Take a square piece of paper, and fold the right edges to the midline. Fold the dashed lines . . .

4. Fold the upper portion down. Crease the left tip on the dashed line.

5. Open the tip up at the crease. Crease the dashed line and open tip to the right. Crease the dashed line . . .

2. . . . to the middle again. Fold the dashed lines . . .

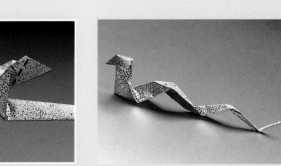

10. Shape the tail further if you wish.

Stag

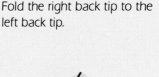

2. Fold the right back tip to the left back tip.

You'll need two pieces of paper for this project. Paper B should be one fourth the size of paper A.

Body

1. Fold paper A following steps 1–11 of the Owl (pages 14–15). Point the open end to the left.

3. Fold upper front half at the midline onto the lower half. Crease the left front wing at the dashed line . . .

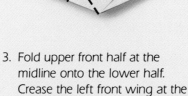

4. . . . first down . . .

5. . . . then up.

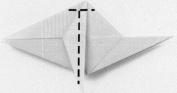

6. Now lift up left tip and push the creases together so the tip stands up.

7. Fold it down. Fold the vertical dashed line . . .

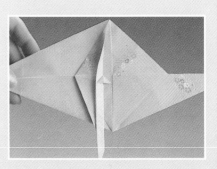

8. . . . to the left of the triangle. Flatten this triangle, and fold the other dashed line that was just created. . .

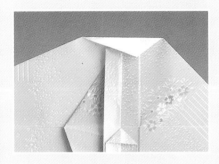

9. . . . in the upper corner (it has already begun to be pulled down).

10. Turn the form over, and fold the upper top wing down.

11. Repeat steps 4 and 5 with left wing.

12. . . . as shown.

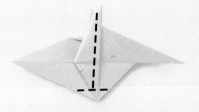

13. Fold the dashed line . . .

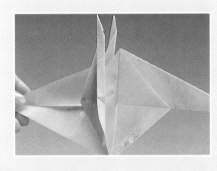

14. . . . to the left.

15. Flatten the little triangle and fold the lower corner up.

16. Open both wings to the middle.

Antlers

17. Follow steps 1–7 of the Sea Lion (page 22) and fold paper B. Point the wing tips to the left.

18. Fold right edges to the middle. Fold the dashed lines . . .

19. . . . forward at the right tip and back along the edges.

20. Turn form over . . .

21. . . . and push the blunt tip underneath the small wing of the body as shown. Glue in place.

22. Fold the upper portion of form back.

23. Turn right tip down on the dashed line . . .

24. . . . and open the left tip on the dashed line.

25. Open the front left tip the left. This is the head.

26. Fold tip of head a little to the inside. Fold dashed line 1 . . .

27. . . . (from step 25) to the right to form the ears. Fold line 2 . . .

28. . . . to the right and open the fold. Turn up line 3 again . . .

29. . . . to form the antler.

30. Fold front legs on line 1 . . .

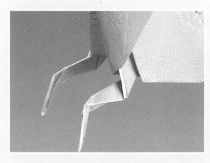

31. . . . to the left, and fold down on line 2.

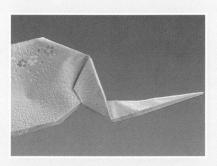

32. Fold tip of back legs on line 3 (from step 30) to the right . . .

33. . . . and fold line 4 down.

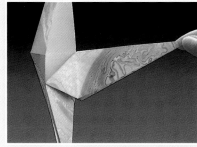

4. . . . and fold the triangle under the lower wing; then . . .

5. . . . do the same on the other side. Fold the dashed line . . .

Lion

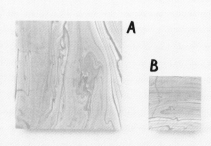

You'll need two pieces of paper for this project. Paper B should be about one fourth the size of paper A.

6. . . . and open the upper tip to the left. Crease dashed lines 1 and 2.

Front portion

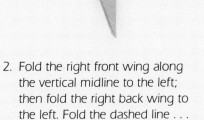

2. Fold the right front wing along the vertical midline to the left; then fold the right back wing to the left. Fold the dashed line . . .

1. Fold paper A. Follow steps 1–11 of the Owl (pages 14–15) and point the open tip up.

3. . . . and open the outer wing to the right. Open left wing on the long right side . . .

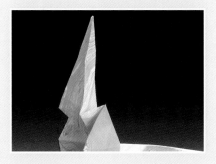

7. Open up the tip on line 1 . . .

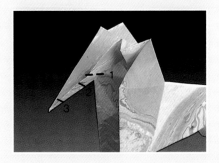

8. . . . and open line 2 to the left.
Crease dashed lines 1, 2 and 3.

12. Crease the front legs at dashed lines 1 and 2.

16. . . . opening line 1 to the right and . . .

9. Open the tip up on line 1, . . .

13. Open both legs up and to the right of crease 1 . . .

17. . . . opening line 2 to the left.
Open tip to the inside slightly.

10. . . . open the tip down on line 2 . . .

14. . . . and at crease 2 open the form down again.

18. Crease right tip and . . .

11. . . . and open the tip to the left on line 3. Fold the tip a little to the inside.

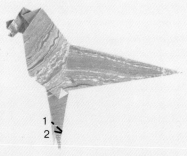

15. Form front paws by creasing along dashed lines 1 and 2 and then by . . .

19. . . . open it to the inside. This is the tail.

Hind quarters

20. Crease paper B diagonally as shown.

21. Fold both upper edges to the middle, vertically (keep the white side inside).

22. Fold both lower edges up to the middle.

23. Fold form together in the middle.

24. Place B under A as shown.

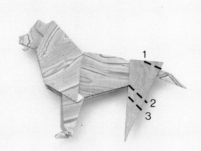

25. Fold B in half, and crease it on the dashed lines.

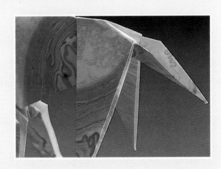

26. Open crease 1 to the inside, and glue B into A.

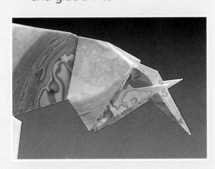

27. Fold the leg up at crease 2 and . . .

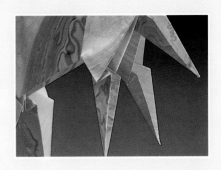

28. . . . crease line 3 down.

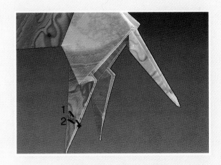

29. Open the tail to the outside. Crease dashed lines 1 and 2 . . .

30. . . . and open crease 1 to the right and crease 2 to the left.

31. Open tips to the inside slightly and your lion is ready to roar.

55

5. Reinforce folds, turn the form over . . .

6. . . . and repeat steps 3 and 5 on this side. Point the open portion of form up. Crease along the dashed lines.

Lioness

1. Fold a square piece of paper along the dashed lines.

3. Lift up the left half of form as shown . . .

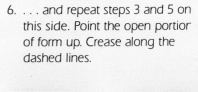

7. Lift up the *entire* left top wing. . .

2. Fold the paper in half, keeping the white side inside.

4. . . . and fold it down flat into a square.

8. . . . open it up . . .

9. . . . and fold it down flat. Fold the entire small right wing . . .

10. . . . to the left.

11. Lift up and open the entire right front wing and fold it down flat.

12. Turn form over and repeat steps 6–11. Crease along the dashed lines.

13. Fold down both upper front edges to the middle; then unfold them.

14. Slowly pull open the horizontal edge of the front wing (the one you folded in step 12) . . .

15. . . . and push right and left corners inside to the middle, vertically.

16. Reinforce the folds; then fold the small triangle . . .

17. . . . up.

18. Repeat steps 13–17 on all four sides. You should have a rhombus with two tips on the left and two on the right. Cut on the dashed line . . .

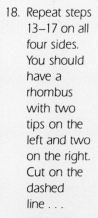

19. . . . into the front wing . . .

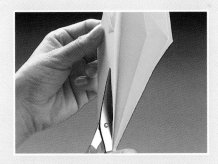

20. . . . as shown. However, do not cut the inner wings.

21. Turn the form around so the cuts you just made are pointing up. Crease the form on the dashed lines and . . .

25. . . . to the inside on both sides.

29. Fold the small triangle up in the middle . . .

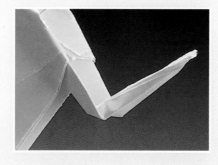

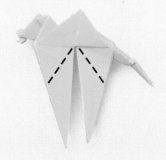

22. . . . open the right tip to the right and the left tip to the left. Fold the dashed line . . .

26. Open dashed line 2 (in step 24) up and . . .

30. . . . on both sides. Fold on the dashed lines . . .

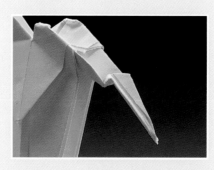

23. . . . to the inside on both sides.

27. . . . open on line 3 down.

31. . . . and open the left lower tip to the left and right lower tip to the right. Open dashed line 1 . . .

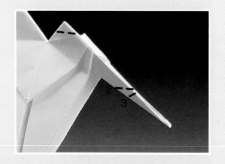

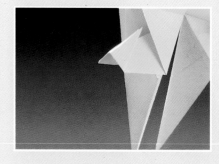

24. Fold dashed line 1 . . .

28. To make the head, fold the left tip, following steps 6–11 of the lion (page 53–54).

32. . . . to the right and . . .

33. . . . open line 2 back to the left.

37. . . . to the inside.

41. . . . down and to the left.

34. Open the right tip on line 3 (see step 31) down and . . .

38. Turn over form. Open the tips on the dashed lines . . .

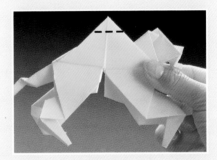

42. Fold both tips a little to the inside. Fold the triangles along the dashed line . . .

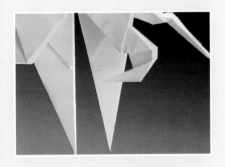

35. . . . open line 4 to the left.

39. . . . to the left and right respectively. Open the left tip at dashed line 1 . . .

43. . . . down on both sides.

36. Fold both tips a little to the inside. Open both the small corners in the middle . . .

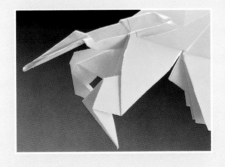

40. . . . to the right. Open the right tip at dashed line 2 . . .

44. To finish your lioness fold these triangles down on both sides.

59

FANTASY
WORLD

5. Open up left tip. Cut the upper layer as shown. Fold along dashed line 2 . . .

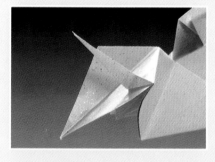

6. . . . as shown.

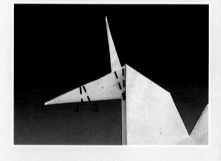

Unicorn

1. Follow steps 1–20 for the Lioness (pages 58–59). Point the tip with the cut wings up. Open the tips along the dashed lines . . .

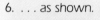

3. . . . inside on both sides. Open the right tip down on dashed line 2 and . . .

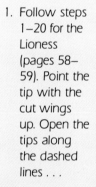

7. Fold the two sides together again. Push along dashed line 1 . . .

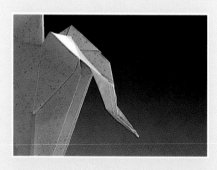

2. . . . to the right (on the right tip) and left (on the left tip). Fold dashed line 1 . . .

4. . . . open the tip to the right on line 3.

8. . . . to the right on both sides up to line 2.

9. Open the tip on line 3 to the right and on line 4 to the left; then fold the tip a little to the inside.

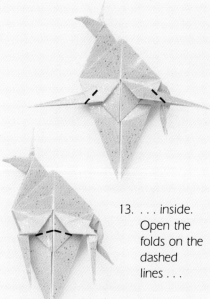

10. Fold small triangle in the center . . .

13. . . . inside. Open the folds on the dashed lines . . .

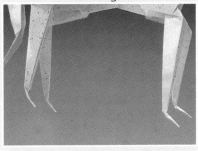

17. Follow steps 12–14 and form the other two legs.

14. . . . down. Fold the dashed lines . . .

18. Open the tips of all four legs slightly to the right.

11. . . . up. Turn the form over and re-peat. Open the tips along the dashed lines . . .

15. . . . so both small corners go to the inside.

19. Fold down the tops of both triangles.

12. . . . to the left and right. Open both tips and fold their lower edges . . .

16. Turn the form over.

20. Fold both triangles down. Fold in the small corners on the right half of the back portion and your unicorn is finished.

5. Fold the left front wing to the right. Turn the form over and repeat.

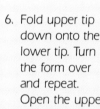

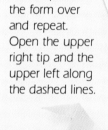

6. Fold upper tip down onto the lower tip. Turn the form over and repeat. Open the upper right tip and the upper left along the dashed lines.

Pegasus

1. Follow steps 1–18 of the Lioness (pages 57–58) but don't cut. Point the open tip up. Fold the left front wing to the right. Cut the dashed line . . .

3. Fold both right front wings to the left, and repeat step 2 again, cutting the lower front wing on the dashed line.

7. Open dashed line 1 . . .

4. Point the cut wings up.

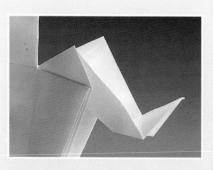

2. . . . on the front lower wing only. Turn the form around and again, cut only the very front wing up to the middle.

8. . . . up. Fold line 2 . . .

9. . . . to the inside on both sides.
    This is the tail.

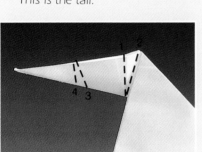

10. Fold dashed line 1 . . .

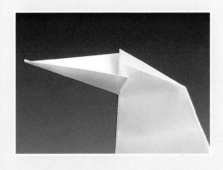

11. . . . to the outside on both
    sides—right up to line 2.

12. Fold line 3 to the outside on
    both sides—right up to line 4.
    Fold the tip to the inside a little.

13. Fold the
    front wing
    and the
    small triangle
    underneath . . .

14. . . . up on
    both sides.
    Open both
    lower tips on
    the dashed
    lines . . .

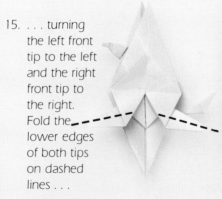

15. . . . turning
    the left front
    tip to the left
    and the right
    front tip to
    the right.
    Fold the
    lower edges
    of both tips
    on dashed
    lines . . .

16. . . . to the inside on both sides.
    On dashed lines 1 and 2 . . .

17. . . . open the front left and right
    tips down.

18. On dashed lines 3 and 4 (in
    step 16) open both tips to the
    right.

19. On line 5 (in step 16) open the
    small corners up and inside.

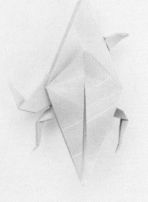

20. Turn the form over . . .

21. . . . and repeat steps 14–19 with both lower tips. Fold the upper corner of the small triangle down along the dashed line.

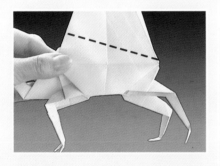

22. Fold the front triangle down to the midline as shown; then turn the form over and repeat.

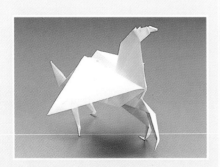

23. To finish, fold down both wings of the Pegasus a little.

Dinosaur

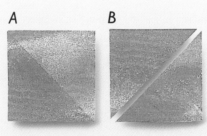

Two pieces of paper are needed for this project. Paper B should be a triangle, and one half the size of A.

Back portion

1. Fold paper A following steps 1–11 of the Owl (pages 14–15). Point the open tip to the left.

2. Pull both right tips apart as shown until . . .

66

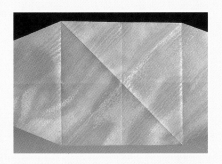

3. . . . the paper is completely flat.

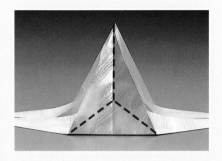

4. Turn the form over. Push both free tips together, folding along the dashed lines.

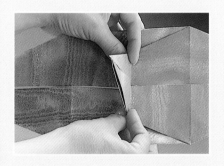

5. Reinforce all folds from the top down to the surface and . . .

6. . . . fold both over to the left.

7. Turn form over. Fold dashed line 1 . . .

8. . . . to the right as shown. Fold dashed line 2 to the middle.

9. Fold lower half of form up. Open the small wing on the dashed line . . .

10. . . . down. Turn the form over, and repeat. Fold on dashed line 1 and push it . . .

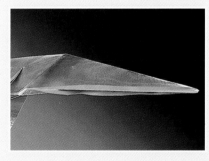

11. . . . to the inside on both sides up to line 2.

Front portion

12. Crease paper B in the middle.

13. Fold the lower corners up to the upper corners (keep the white side inside).

14. Fold the upper edges down to the middle vertically.

15. Open the left half of the form and turn the crease to the inside.

16. Repeat step 15 on the right half of the form, and fold down the upper tips. Fold the dashed lines . . .

17. . . . back to the middle. Fold the form in the middle and push the neck on both sides along dashed line 1 . . .

21. Open the tip at the crease to the outside and back again a little to the inside.

23. . . . and glue as shown. Open the foot on dashed line 1 . . .

18. . . . to the inside and up to line 2.

22. Push both forms together . . .

24. . . . to the right and on line 2 . . .

19. Open the legs on line 3 up and open them again on line 4 down.

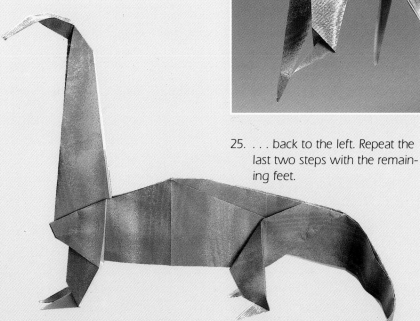

25. . . . back to the left. Repeat the last two steps with the remaining feet.

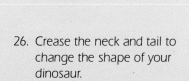

20. Open the upper tip at line 5 (in step 17). Crease the dashed line.

26. Crease the neck and tail to change the shape of your dinosaur.

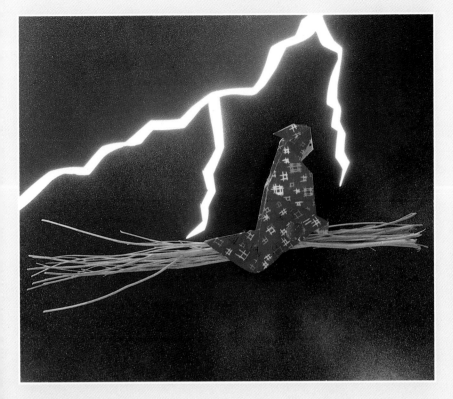

5. . . . again to the right. Crease the dashed lines.

6. Fold the right corners inside at the creases; then . . .

Witch

7. . . . turn the form over and repeat. Open the lower tip on the dashed line . . .

1. Fold a square piece of paper . . .

3. . . . to the right. Fold dashed line 1 . . .

2. . . . diagonally. (Keep the white side outside.) Fold both edges on the dashed line . . .

4. . . . to the left and line 2 to the right. Open the dashed line . . .

8. . . . to the left. Set your witch on a broom and she will be ready to fly.

THE ZOO

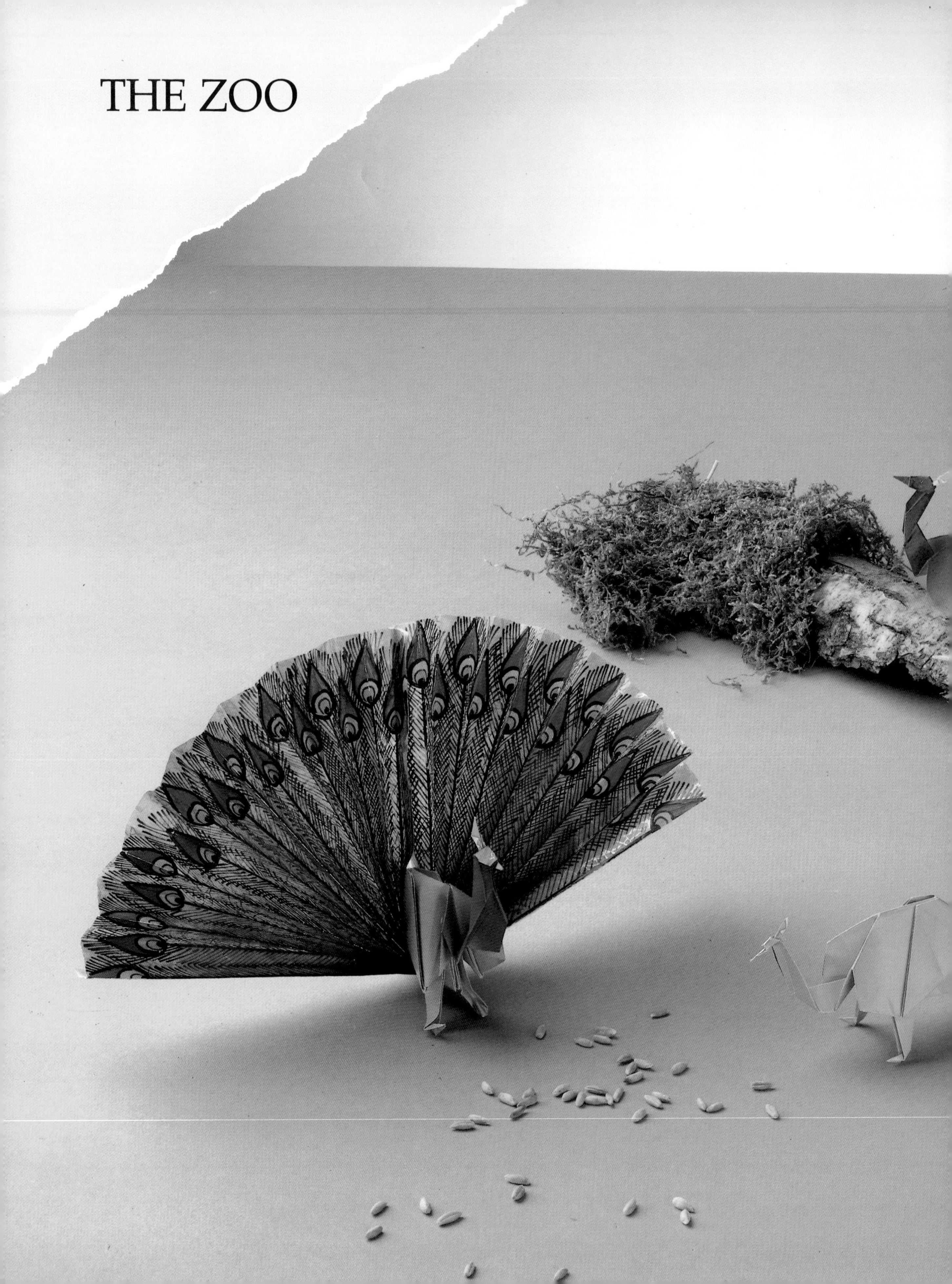

5. Open the left half and pull the tip up.

6. Fold the left half together again and flatten the form.

Squirrel

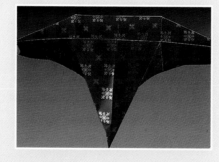

1. Follow steps 1–11 for the Owl (pages 14–15). Point the open tip to the left. Carefully pull . . .

3. Fold the form together in the middle and . . .

7. Repeat steps 5 and 6 with the right half of the form. Fold both right tips on dashed line 1 . . .

8. . . . to either side of the middle. Open the left tip to the left on dashed line 2. Fold the tip along the dashed line . . .

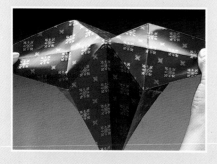

2. . . . the right tips apart.

4. . . . fold down both sides until smooth.

9. . . . to the right; then open the tip of the head upwards.

13. . . . forward and backwards, respectively. Open both tips on the dashed line . . .

14. . . . up. Open both tips on dashed line 1 . . .

17. Open the tail on dashed line 1 . . .

18. . . . to the right; . . .

10. Cut the tip in the middle. Fold both corners along the dashed lines . . .

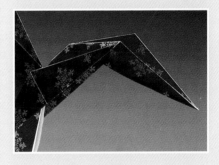

11. . . . to the inside.

15. . . . down.

19. . . . on line 2 down and to the right, and . . .

12. Fold both the right wings of the form . . .

16. Fold dashed line 2 (from step 10) to the inside.

20. . . . on line 3 down again.

4. Fold down the top wing.

5. Fold the right half over.

6. Temporarily fold up the feet (do not crease!). Crease the lower tip along the dashed line and . . .

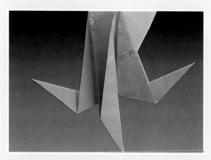

7. . . . open it to the outside. This is the tail.

Kangaroo (and Baby)

1. Follow steps 1–7 for the Squirrel (page 72). Point the open tip up. Fold . . .

2. . . . the left top wing over; then turn the form over and repeat. Open along the dashed lines . . .

3. . . . to the right and left respectively. These are the feet.

8. Fold the feet down again. Crease along the dashed line . . .

12. . . . and open the left tip and the right corners inside.

16. Crease both dashed lines and push corner on line 1 . . .

9. . . . and open the tip to the left. Crease the dashed line . . .

13. Unfold the form in the middle . . .

17. . . . down to line 2.

10. . . . and open the tip back to the right. Crease the dashed line . . .

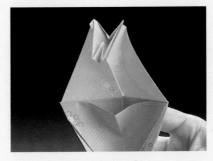

14. . . . and pull out pouch from the inside.

18. Pull out both corners a little.

11. . . . and open the tip back to the left. Crease both dashed lines . . .

15. Fold the form together again.

19. Fold a smaller square to make a baby kangaroo and let it snuggle safely into its mother's pouch.

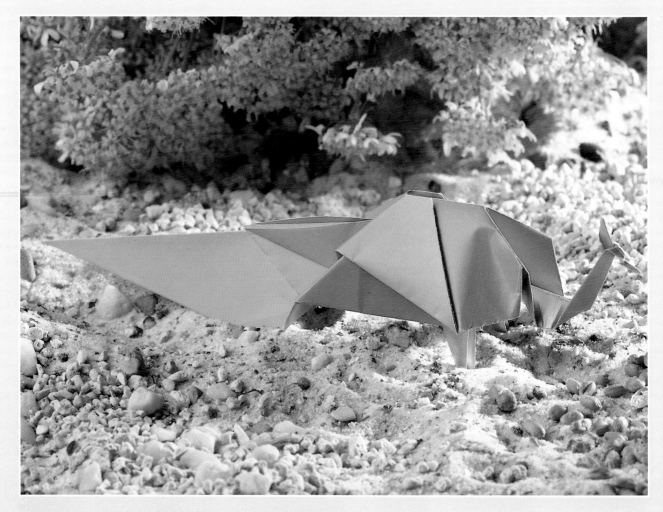

Peacock with Tail Folded

1. Follow steps 1–11 for the Owl (pages 14–15). Point the open end to the left.

3. Fold the two left tips over to the middle, along the dashed line.

5. . . . up . . .

2. Fold the right wing to the left.

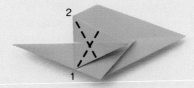

4. Crease on dashed line 1 . . .

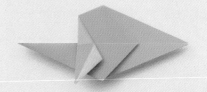

6. . . . and on line 2 down.

7. Now lift the tip up and push it together at the creases in the middle and . . .

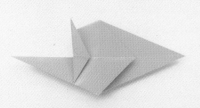

8. . . . fold it up.

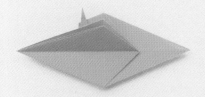

9. Fold both left wings up.

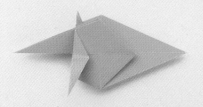

10. Repeat steps 4–7 with the left tip and fold the tip down. Fold the upper front wing . . .

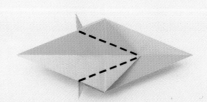

11. . . . down. Fold along the dashed lines . . .

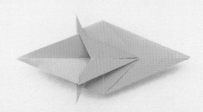

12. . . . to the middle, horizontally.

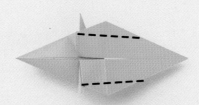

13. Turn form over. Fold the dashed lines . . .

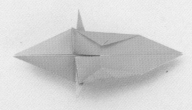

14. . . . down and up, respectively. Fold the upper portion of the form . . .

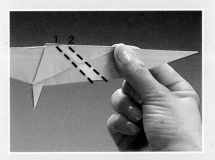

15. . . . down. Open the tip down on dashed line 1 . . .

16. . . . and up on line 2.

17. Open the left tip on the dashed line . . .

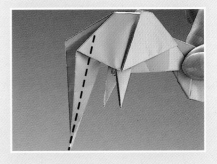

18. . . . down. Crease the edges on the dashed line.

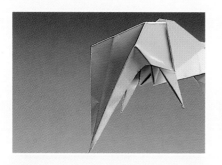

19. Open the corner down.

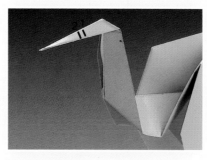

23. . . . to the left again. This will form the head. Fold line 1 . . .

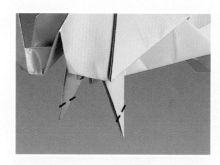

25. Open dashed line and . . .

20. Fold the creases from step 18 in half, turning the corners inside. Open the tip to the left on dashed line 1 . . .

24. . . . to the inside and line 2 to the outside. This is the beak.

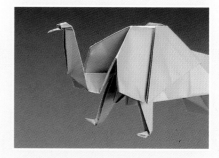

26. . . . turn both legs to the left.

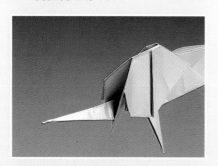

21. . . . and up on line 2.

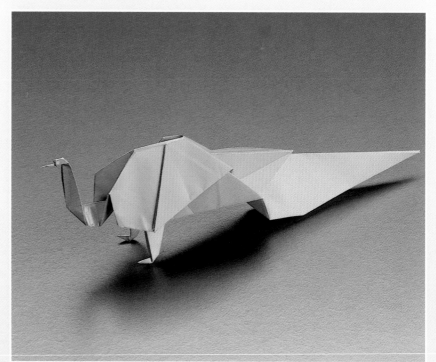

27. If you want, you may add a crown to the head of the bird.

22. Open the tip on the dashed line . . .

4. . . . follow steps 17–27 for the Peacock with Tail Folded. This is the body of the bird.

Tail

5. Fold the second paper accordion-fashion.

Peacock with Tail Unfolded

Two identical square pieces of paper are needed for this project.

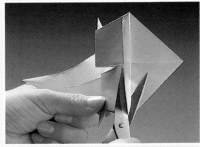

2. . . . cut off the right front wing.

6. Fold it together to form a fan, glue to the body as shown and . . .

Body

1. Follow steps 1–13 of the Peacock with Tail Folded (page 77) with one piece. On the dashed line . . .

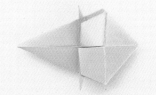

3. Fold the form and . . .

7. . . . glue the inner edges together.

INDEX